SOLO FLITE

An Alaska Puppy Becomes a Legend

by **Marianne Schlegelmilch**

illustrated by **David W. Large Jr.**

ISBN 1-888125-94-2

Library of Congress Catalog Card Number: 2002108327

Book design by David W. Large Jr.
Edited by Margaret Baker

~ First Edition 2002 ~

Published by Blood Bank of Alaska
4000 Laurel Street
Anchorage, Alaska 99508
(907) 563-3110

Manufactured in the United States of America.

Dedication

SOLO FLITE is dedicated to the spirit of Alaska, its people and their dogs. In writing this book, I honor my dog of 14 years, Solo, and thank her for the years of joy that she brought into my life. I thank my husband, Bill, for his significant contribution to this story and for his love and support. Finally, I thank the Blood Bank of Alaska for helping bring my story to print and the family of Joe Redington Sr. for their support and for exemplifying the best of Alaska's people.

~ Marianne Schlegelmilch

I dedicate this book to Dee Boyles and Hugh McPeck for their inspiration and wisdom as mentors. I would also like to thank my mom, dad, and sister for their support over the years. I would like to thank my wonderful friend and significant other, Beatriz Oms for all her help and simply for taking a little time out of her day to put up with me. Finally, I would like to thank the Blood Bank of Alaska for giving me the opportunity to work on this project, especially Thomas Hathaway, Gregg Schomaker, Marianne Schlegelmilch, and Margaret Baker.

~ David W. Large Jr

Foreword by Vi Redington
Wife of Joe Redington Sr.
Father of the Iditarod

I'm sure Joe would have approved and enjoyed this story, as it will appeal to both children and adults and especially because it is told from the dog's point of view. Here you get a feel for the joy and excitement of dog mushing as well as the trust and affections between the musher and his or her dogs.

Vi Redington

Thanks Joe for helping me realize my dream
Rick Swenson

Thank you Joe! For sharing your dream with us. I love you!
DeeDee Jonrowe "Your Student"

Thanks, Joe You've made all of us famous and our dreams come true.
Doug F. Swingley

Good Job Joe
Charlie Boulding

ITS A GREAT RACE JOE THANK YOU SONNY LINDNER

Happy Trails Joe on all your travels past and present!
Martin Buser

Thank you, Joe for what you have done with our Best Friends, DOGS! We love you!
Mitch Willis

Thank you Joe Wonderful Dream
John Baker

Thanks to Joe for a dream come true
Jeff King Denali, Alaska

See you on the trail Joe.
Mitch Seavey

Wonderful he had done
Gerald Riley

Thank you Joe for giving us a dream to follow
Ramy Blood

Following is a family tradition
Ray Redington 2002

Blood Bank of Alaska
IN MEMORY OF JOE REDINGTON, SR. 1917-1999
"Supporter and recipient of blood services from the Blood Bank of Alaska"

Thanks Joe for always leading the way. We will miss you!
Linwood

Thanks Joe for the last great Race
Hans Gatt

Thanks for everything Joe, you're the man!
Tim Osmar

Carried by:
Martin Buser
Iditarod 2002

Sled # 14   Finishing Place: 1st

Solo rolled on his back in the dog lot as the last tour bus pulled away from the kennel. He had romped and played all day, entertaining the tourists who had come to see a real sled dog. It was 9 PM and the sun was still fairly high on the horizon as he lay there pondering his new name. Until the day before, he had answered to "Lttle Fur Ball" or "Boy."

He thought back to the night before when Joe had thrown him a leftover piece of salmon after nearly stepping on him on the way out the door. They had been together ever since Joe had found him alone and frightened on the Iditarod trail just north of Knik Lake near his homestead outside Wasilla, Alaska. "I think I'll call you Solo," Joe had said nonchalantly. "Solo Flite."

Solo pondered the meaning of his new name, "Is it because I am so small?"

One of Joe's sons had been overheard laughing and saying that the puppy was "so low he had to look up to see down!"

"Is that my name? So Low?" he thought. "That's not cool. So Low is definitely not cool!" Or maybe it was because he didn't have any brothers or sisters. All the other puppies had plenty of brothers and sisters and never seemed to run out of playmates. "Hmmmm," he thought. "I'll bet that's exactly how I got this name. Solo Flite – it has style."

The fireweed was just coming into bloom when Joe scooped Solo in his arms one day and loaded him into the cockpit for a flight to Skwentna. It was going to be a quick trip to pick up some supplies left there from last year's Iditarod race, and then back home before dinner. Joe, like many mushers, waited until the good weather of summer to recover supplies from the many drop zones along the 1000-mile trail. Solo had never been in a plane before, but he had seen Joe and others in his family in it many times.

"The fireweed was just coming into bloom when Joe scooped Solo in his arms one day..."

At first Solo was frightened as the plane rumbled and tilted left, then right, before leveling off above the treetops. Finally, getting up the courage to peek out of the window, he could see what looked like a narrow road winding among lakes and rivers for as far as he could see. "See that, Boy?" said Joe. "That's the Iditarod Trail. Some day you and I are going to run that trail all the way to Nome."

"Nome?" Solo thought, "I wonder where Nome is?" He laid his head on the seat, put a paw over his nose, and let himself enjoy the smoothness of the flight as the sun shining through the cockpit window warmed his back. He didn't know how much time had passed before the plane jerked and the hum of the engine turned into a series of snorts and chortles.

"Hold on, Solo," Joe whispered, "We're going to have to land in the trees." The sound of leaves and branches scraping along the sides of the plane, followed by a roll to the left and a dip forward, made Solo tuck his tail between his legs and cover his face with both front paws. When everything was still, he looked up. Through the window the ground appeared sort of sideways, but not too far below. He looked over at Joe and saw him rubbing a bump on his head. "Well, at least we didn't put a hole in her," Joe said as he climbed out the window and jumped to the ground, then reached up to check the prop. Joe was going to be busy for a while trying to bend the tip of the prop blade straight again.

Solo looked around the cockpit considering his options, "Guess I'll try to climb down this tree and wait for Joe."

Crawling out of the plane proved to be just a little bit difficult. Solo slid off the fuselage and tumbled down, bouncing over a couple of birch branches before landing under a spruce bough flat on his belly with all four feet sticking straight from his sides. "Whew! That was close!" he said as he looked up, raising himself to all fours and shaking off the fall. No one had told him that dogs couldn't climb trees.

"*He laid his head on the seat, put a paw over his nose, and let himself enjoy the smoothness of the flight...*"

Almost immediately, Solo saw a little fur ball under the birch tree right beside him. "I wonder who that is?" The fur ball ignored Solo as it munched on the new shoots surrounding the birch tree trunk. Solo inched closer and came around behind it, trying to pick up its scent. Joe's voice boomed out at the same time Solo felt the sharp twang in his nose: "Watch out for that porcupine, Solo!"

The needle-like jab made Solo jump, lose his balance, and tumble to the ground. He landed squarely at the feet of a huge raven, who flapped his wings anxiously trying to get out of the way. The two of them danced around in a frenzied circle for several minutes. Finally, the bird flew up to a branch above, giving Solo time to stop and rest. "Ouch!" The pain in Solo's nose was getting worse, and from the corner of his eye, he could see something long and pointed sticking out from his face.

"Sit still, young puppy," the raven said as he flew down, landing next to the shivering little dog. Solo started backing away. "Please sit still!" cawed the bird. Solo was too frightened to move. The raven was huge! Solo's eyes grew wider as the bird's giant beak came closer to his nose and gently plucked the sharp quill. "Now you will be okay," the raven said. The pain was gone. Solo felt better already.

"*Who* are you?" Solo asked.

"My name is Spirit. I am the guardian of the people born in this region," the bird answered.

"Well, thank you for helping me," Solo replied.

"You're welcome, little puppy friend," Spirit said as he spread his magnificent wings and flew off toward the mountains.

"My name is Spirit. I am the guardian of the people born in this region," the bird answered.

Solo was exhausted from his ordeal. Since Joe was still busy fixing the bent propeller, Solo curled up against a rock and fell asleep to the sound of the water rushing over the rocks in a nearby stream. He slept all afternoon and all night while Joe worked on the plane. When he awoke, the morning sun was brightening the horizon. Solo stood up, gingerly licked the dew droplets off his wounded nose, and shook himself awake. Looking around, he could see that Joe had straightened the propeller and had somehow managed to loosen most of the spruce boughs that had been holding the plane sideways. The engine started easily. Joe lowered the wheels and generated enough traction to taxi across the clearing. Solo was excited. By then he was feeling mighty hungry, and it looked like they would be ready to leave soon. As he started toward the plane, he was startled by the sound of branches snapping behind him. He had no time to react to the roar of a bear sow before she slapped him and sent him flying through the air straight for the creek.

Joe saw the attack, but there was little he could do. The bear sow was only trying to protect her cubs when the noise of the plane startled them out into the clearing right beside Solo. As Solo landed in the creek, the sow turned and took off after Joe, whose only hope of escape was to rev up the engine and try to get airborne. The wheels of the airplane lifted off the ground just as the sow was about to bite a hole in the tail of the plane. Looking down, Joe could see no sign of Solo. He circled the clearing repeatedly until the fuel gauge was almost empty. The angry sow and her cubs continued to guard the clearing. Joe needed to refuel, so he decided he would have to come back for Solo later.

"...the sow had turned and taken off after Joe, whose only hope of escape was to rev up the engine and try to get airborne."

What Joe didn't know was that Solo, after climbing out of the creek, had found his way to an old cabin on the other side. He managed to crawl through a small hole in the door and had no plans to come back out until he was dry and the sow and her cubs were gone. Besides, there was food in the cabin – cereal and a piece of dried salmon. Solo ate his fill. Feeling full and safe, he slept soundly for three days. He didn't hear Joe return, circling for hours over the clearing. He didn't even know that the sow and her two cubs had come within 50 feet of the cabin before moving on.

He heard nothing until Harry Conroy's strong hands lifted him into his arms saying, "Well, look at this! What do we have here? Looks like a little burglar puppy."

"I'm no burglar! I'm no burglar!" Solo barked, jumping into Harry's lap and wagging his tail.

"Well, let's give you a name, 'cause it looks like you're coming back to the kennel with me," Harry said as he scratched Solo's ears.

Solo put his paws over his nose and thought, "Here we go with the name thing again." But to Solo's surprise, Harry looked him right in the eye and said, "I think your name will be Solo in honor of your being left here all alone." Then he tucked Solo in his pack for the long hike back to the bluff where his plane was waiting.

Conroy kennels were located on the west side of Fairbanks and had a reputation for being the best in the area. Harry was a retired veterinarian, who had come to Alaska to race sled dogs. So far, he had twice finished the shorter but more difficult Yukon Quest sled dog race. He was entered as a rookie in the Iditarod, the biggest race of his life.

Harry was counting on Sela to help him finish in the top 20. Sela was strong and determined, and she had come a long way from the devastated state he had found her in six months earlier. Harry had landed his plane in a clearing and walked to Joe Redington's homestead to buy some sleds that Joe was selling. On his way back to the plane, Harry heard a faint whimper coming from just off the trail. When he finally found Sela lying in the weeds, she couldn't lift her head and was bleeding from her mouth. Her mate, Teddy, lay lifeless beside her. From the moose prints close to the two dogs, Harry could see that Teddy had been trampled, probably while trying to protect Sela. What Harry didn't know was that Sela had survived only by playing dead while their puppy ran into the woods farther down the trail. Harry scooped Sela up into his arms, loaded her into one of the sleds, and pulled her back to his plane for the flight back to Fairbanks.

He nursed her back to health and slowly increased her exercise every day until she was stronger than ever. Harry knew he had a winner in Sela. "Solo would be in good hands," Harry thought, as he brought the puppy to her. "Sela, I brought you someone to look after. His name is Solo and he needs a little TLC." He opened the pen and placed a wide-eyed Solo inside. Solo let out a soft little woof before curling up in the corner of the kennel with his head between his front paws. Sela looked him over for a quick moment, then nudged him to her food bowl. Sela backed away to let Solo eat. Taking her cue, he ate his first real meal in days and settled down for a long sleep next to Sela.

*S*ummer gave way to fall as Solo flourished under Sela's watchful eye. Solo practiced her focused discipline, copying her as she overcame her injuries and grew strong. Solo himself had grown into sixty pounds of muscled energy. His puppy coat had long ago been replaced with the sleek coat of his husky heritage. Sela watched him grow and helped him learn to channel his juvenile energy. Solo was emerging not only as a strong team player, but also as a leader. Often, while watching him, she thought of Teddy. Teddy had displayed the same confident, yet easygoing nature that she saw in Solo. She couldn't quite figure out what it was, but Solo was special.

Late one morning, Sela and Solo were just returning from a trail run. Harry had unharnessed them about a mile from the kennel, and they were running along the trail enjoying the brisk October air when they saw a moose ahead. Solo watched Sela freeze in place, unaware that she was paralyzed with the memory of that day on the trail when Teddy had lost his life trying to protect his family. Watching Sela, Solo felt unexpected fear swell inside. Courage he never knew he had propelled him forward. The hair on his back stood on end as he bared his fangs and growled at the moose. Solo lunged, nipping its heels. The moose stomped angrily, trying to make a hoof crash against Solo's body. The two of them danced in a vicious circle for a few minutes until the moose ran off into the woods.

"It was late morning and Sela and Solo were just returning from a trail run. ...they were running along the trail enjoying the brisk October air when they saw a moose ahead."

Sela stood stunned! The resemblance was unmistakable – the way he cocked his head, the little skip in his gait, the prancing trot, the white-tipped tail held high. She wondered why she hadn't seen it before. Everything made sense then. No wonder the moose had evoked such a strong reaction in Solo. Sela, filled with emotion, looked up at Solo. She spoke to him softly as he walked toward her, "Solo, I'm your mother."

Sela and Solo wandered into the dog lot way after dark. "There you two are!" a frantic Harry scolded them as he poured them some fresh water. "I was just about ready to send Wolf out looking for you." Both Sela and Solo hung their heads, sad at disappointing Harry. They could barely look at Wolf, who was just as happy to not be pressed into action. He had spent many a night helping Harry track down one dog or another and now that he was 10, he preferred to go to sleep when the sun did. Instantly softened by Solo's bowed head and hesitant gait, Wolf circled the bedding in his sleeping area and lay down. "Good night, kids," he growled as he tucked his nose under his right front paw, "Glad you made it back okay."

"Good night, Wolf," said Solo.

The next two months were a blur of activity. Harry drew 29th place for the start out of the 80 mushers entered in that year's race. He was feeling confident, not only that he would finish, but also that he would be the first rookie to win the Iditarod. Sela was turning out to be a strong leader, and Harry was almost sure that she would be his lead dog. It was early November when Harry made the final decision. Solo sat quietly with the others as Harry named his team. Sela would be his lead dog. Having made that decision, picking the other 11 was easy. Solo's ears were raised as Harry's voice called out the names of the rest of the team: "Annie, Sam, Skat, Ember, Mac, Bootle, Jewel, Target, Dell, Boge, and Solo."

"Did he say Solo? Dell, did he say Solo? Target, did you hear all the names?" Solo was jumping up and down and running back and forth behind the rest of the dogs in excited disbelief.

"Solo, my son, you are not hearing things," said Sela. "You have trained well, and you have earned your place on our team."

"Wow!" yipped Solo. "I can't believe I'm going to be an Iditarod dog!" Everyone stared as Solo ran in a circle and then did a full summersault landing right at Harry's feet. Harry laughed as he scooped Solo into his arms and tossed him playfully back on the ground.

"Looks like you've got enough enthusiasm for all of us," Harry said as he led the team back to their kennels and bedded them down for the night. It was nearly dawn before Solo could quit thinking of the race and finally fell asleep.

Solo was still in a state of disbelief when he hooked up for training the next day. He learned that he would be paired with Dell and that they would be the fourth team back. Sela would run as the lone leader, and Bootle would run as the stand-alone between the pairs Dell/Solo and Jewel/Target. Solo had always admired Dell and felt that he would be a great teammate. Dell, an Iditarod veteran, had developed respect for Solo, and he knew that Solo would be a strong, loyal teammate. Together they tackled their training with so much determination that Harry seemed more convinced by the day that he had made the right choice, both in picking Solo for the team and in pairing him with Dell.

*T*raining for the race was harder than Solo had anticipated. Harry was patient and kind, making Solo and the team members want to live up to his expectations. Still, the weather made training difficult. The lack of snow make it seem darker than usual and temperatures hovered just above zero during the day. In the morning the trails were icy, and the short days meant that it was nearly noon before they could run the trail and close to 2 PM when they had to stop. Solo had to learn to run in booties, and he had to learn to run without them. Sela taught him a few tricks about running on the hard, frozen trail, but Solo felt relieved for his sore feet when the snow started to fall right before Christmas.

Harry seemed happy to see the snow. Forty inches fell over several days, so Harry had his hands full plowing out the yard. Two days passed before training resumed. The team used that time for much-needed rest and play, and for many of the dogs it was a chance to get used to the snow. Jumping into snowdrifts was Solo's newfound passion. "Come on, Sela," he woofed as he skimmed over the tops of three large drifts before tumbling so deep into a fourth that only the tip of his head was showing. "Come on over and try this! This is fun!" he called as he bounded into the air, shaking off most of the snow before landing on the ground.

"There is still so much puppy in you. You have enough energy to get us all to Nome in record time," Sela teased Solo. Then she chased him until they both fell laughing into the snow.

On Christmas Eve, the Fairbanks snowmachine club groomed the trail and hurried home to prepare for the party at Harry's. Harry lit a big bonfire next to the dog lot, and some of Harry's workers hauled out a huge kettle and hung it over the fire. By 3 PM the moose stew was starting to simmer. Solo and the other dogs watched as friends and family gathered around the fire. Everyone brought food, so there was more than enough to eat. People also brought gifts that were homemade and given out of love and respect. Even the dogs got gifts. Solo chomped down his very first homemade dog biscuit, and he and Dell spent the next hour trying to negotiate a second one. Harry loved the blueberry preserves he got from his friend Sarah Garner. Solo decided that anything that made Harry as happy as Sarah Garner's preserves must be really good, so he sampled them for himself. The next thing he knew both Harry and Sarah were laughing at his purple muzzle and trying to catch him before he could make a big mess. Thinking it was some kind of game, Solo ran like the wind as everyone at the party tried to catch him. Lying in his kennel after the party, Solo could not believe how much purple snow covered Harry's yard! Solo liked the preserves, and he liked Sarah for making Harry look so happy.

It was late January when Sarah's 6th grade sewing class finished the booties for the team. They were made of flame-orange cardura with white Velcro closures. Solo thought they were quite comfortable and especially loved the black raven that was embroidered on the side of each bootie. When the team ran, the ravens looked like they were flying alongside the dogs' feet.

The morning of the Ceremonial Start was bright. The new-fallen snow covering downtown Anchorage sparkled in the sunlight. It was minus ten degrees, so the crowd huddled together to keep warm, parkas zipped all the way to the top. The students were excited, but nervous, as they booted up Harry's team. The preparations for the start went off without a hitch, and soon the team raced through the city streets. The dogs, their boots firmly in place, kicked up snow that shimmered like diamonds.

Harry was pleased with the team's run into the Eagle River checkpoint. The dogs were running just as he had trained them. Harry bedded the team down early, and Solo drifted into sound sleep. He woke around midnight to the crackle of the northern lights. He was excited and nervous about the race, not only for himself, but also for Sela and the rest of the team. He worried about maintaining his strength; he worried about Sela bearing all the pressure of leading. He worried about Harry and hoped his dream of winning could come true. Because the real start of the race would come in only a few more hours, Solo somehow willed himself back to sleep.

Solo did not remember when he woke up if the raven had appeared in his dreams or had really visited him under the aurora, but the recollection was clear either way. It was Spirit, the same raven who had visited him after the plane crash and plucked the porcupine quill from his nose. "It is good to see that you have grown into a fine and strong sled dog," Spirit said. "And it is right that you have found your mother and are joining her team to help your friend Harry win. You will be tested soon, but you will succeed." Spirit plucked one of his feathers and placed it under Solo's collar, and then he flew off into the night as Solo watched quietly .

The restart was exciting. The trail was lined with campfires and campers dressed in the traditional Alaskan winter garb of down, fleece, and fur. The trail was freshly groomed and smooth. The teams traveled one after another down Knik-Goosebay road on the first leg of the race, then veered off across Knik Lake just south of Joe Redington's house, the first home that Solo had ever known.

Just the day before, Solo had learned about Joe's cancer and his death in the spring. He must have gotten sick right after the plane crash. Solo matched pace with the others as the team slowed to allow Harry to throw a tribute of flowers along the trail in front of Joe's house and tip his hat to Joe's widow, Vi, who was standing nearby wearing a purple parka and one of the felt hats she is so famous for. Although sad about Joe's death, Solo felt energized to be so close to his first home again. He remembered the day in the plane when Joe had first told him about the Iditarod Trail. He hoped that Joe was proud of him. The team accelerated and took a hard right at the lake as team after team behind them continued the flower tribute in front of Redington's kennel. They ran until 6 PM, when they pulled into the checkpoint at Yentna for the night.

The weather held for the next four days as the race toward Nome continued. Five mushers had scratched already – four due to technical problems and one due to a broken ankle. Harry and his team were holding steady in 13th place until the fourth day when a sudden sequence of events catapulted them into 7th place. No one knows what happened to cause two of the teams ahead to collide. When their dogs and sleds were finally untangled, both of those teams, headed by veteran Iditarod mushers, were forced to scratch. Three teams stopped for their mandatory layovers, and one fell behind Harry when it stopped to wait for an injured dog to be evacuated.

It wasn't until they arrived in Koyuk that Harry was even aware of their standing in 7th place. In a bold and carefully thought-out move, he pushed the team past two more checkpoints before stopping for his 24-hour layover. When the team pulled out of Golovin a day later, they were in 3rd place.

Just north of White Mountain, the team was caught in a whiteout. Sela and the others were blinded by the swirling snow. Unable to see the trail any longer, they veered slightly off the trail. Without warning, the first five dogs felt themselves sink chest-deep into frigid water. Sela and the others were tangled and treading water. Harry had a deep, three-inch-long cut on the palm of his right hand and was trying to stop the bleeding by wrapping it with a piece of cloth torn out of his parka lining. It was snowing sideways, leaving everyone struggling to maintain direction.

Sela, already exhausted by the race, was quickly becoming hypothermic and needed to be unharnessed and pulled out of the water. Forgetting his own pain and struggling with the use of only his left hand, Harry waded knee-deep into the freezing water, grabbing her by the scruff of her neck. He unhooked the harness and pulled her and then the others onto dry land and managed to build a fire. Once the dogs were warming by the fire, Harry pulled the sled from the water. The right sled runner was cracked, probably caught on the frozen sweeper near the edge of the water. Radio communication had been lost due to the storm, and Harry, his clothes wet and his hand throbbing in pain from the cut, had no choice but to hole up for the night, try to fix the sled, and dry himself and his dogs out.

Solo and the remaining team circled around Sela and the four leaders, doing what they could to help warm them. "Are you okay Mother?" he whispered, afraid for the first time that he might lose Sela again.

"I'm fine son, now go help the others," Sela said, and Solo did. He showed the dry dogs how to lie tightly around those who were wet, checked everyone for injuries, kept them from being afraid, and stopped them from pulling against the sled as Harry tried to fix it. Harry was exhausted as he worked in the dark, fixing the runner with a piece of harness line and duct tape.

Everyone on the team figured the race was lost at that point. To Solo, it no longer seemed important to win. Right then, it was only important to find the trail and get to Nome. Sela was too exhausted and cold to lead, and the front four were in similar condition. Leaving them for later pick-up was out of the question. Harry made his decision while struggling to fix the sled. Only 20 miles from Nome and as close to winning as he had ever dreamed, he emptied his sled of all gear, food, and mandatory race items. One by one he loaded five shivering dogs into his sled, covered them with a tarp, and hooked Solo up as the leader with the remaining dogs behind. "I need you to lead us to Nome, Solo," Harry whispered before falling into exhausted sleep alongside his dogs in the sled.

Solo knew that they were all depending on him. Remembering the words of Spirit and with a confidence that astounded him, he started the team slowly away from the wash. It was then that he saw the first raven appear — first one, then two, three, four, five. One after one, the ravens began landing ahead of him, looking like black lumps of coal marking the trail in the snow. At first the team reluctantly followed Solo as the ravens leapfrogged ahead of him, guiding them slowly along. Solo found himself having to coax the team, who didn't seem to see the ravens. "Don't go, Solo. We'll never make it. You'll only make it worse," he heard the other dogs say. Thinking only of Harry and his teammates, he gently and steadily moved on.

"Can't you see them?" Solo said to the others. "Can't you see the birds?" The raven feather rubbed a little under his harness and a couple of times he could almost imagine Spirit flying alongside him as one by one the other dogs seemed to see the ravens and started chasing them. The dogs jumped and pulled at the harness, tongues hanging out as they tried to catch the birds. At one point, when it was snowing too hard to see the ravens, Solo thought he felt Spirit's wings flap above him, guiding him on.

Harry woke up in bewilderment just as the blizzard was ending. The run to Nome took about eight hours, but it was still light when Solo, Harry, and the team pulled onto Front Street to the biggest crowd gathered in over 15 years. People stood ten-deep from one end of town to the other, and lights from TV cameras made the day even brighter. Solo was exhausted and had lost all but one of his booties. "Hunhh, hunhh, hunhh," he grunted as his breath rose in the frigid air. The finish line was near, but Solo's legs ached so much that he was not sure he could cross it. Nearing collapse, Solo stumbled. Just as he was about to fall nose-first in the snow, he caught a flash of black against the white that made him look up. He saw Spirit, and felt a surge of energy as the raven willed him the strength to pull the team under the Burled Arch.

All of his strength focused ahead, Solo led the entire team across the finish line. They were quickly surrounded by Sarah and her students hugging them and talking at the same time. Jumping from the sled, Harry brushed aside the doctor trying to tend to his hand. A team of veterinarians unloaded Sela and the others from the sled and took them into the temporary clinic for examination and first aid. Harry unhitched an exhausted Solo and carried him under his arm while unhitching his other dogs and handing them over to the volunteers. "You were great Solo," Harry kept saying. "We all owe you our lives." Solo, for his part, was thankful to be in a safe place and happy that everyone on the team had made it.

"It's okay, Harry. It's okay," he panted as he nuzzled his head under Harry's chin. "It's okay." Solo could hardly believe that he had managed to lead the team all the way to Nome.

"So, who won?" Harry asked the race marshall, who approached after Harry had finished tending to his team. "You can mark us as scratched since I threw out my mandatory gear about 20 miles back." While still holding Solo tightly in his arms and not waiting for an answer from the marshall, Harry, brushing aside at least five microphones that had been thrust in his face, walked back to his sled to check the battered runner.

It wasn't until Sarah caught up with him and whispered in his ear that Harry actually stopped in his tracks. Tears welled in his eyes as the race marshall approached again. Solo listened as the race marshall told them what everyone else at the finish already knew. Harry, Solo, Sela and the rest of the team had come in first place. The storm, far worse than they realized, had held all of the other teams back for at least two days. In a move unprecedented in Iditarod history, the judges reached a unanimous decision: Harry's team had indeed won the Iditarod Race in the true spirit that Joe Redington had intended. The judges voted that Harry's team would have been first with or without the storm and that Harry had displayed true courage and heroic judgment in placing the welfare of his team ahead of the race. It was with great pride and honor that Harry was presented the first Joe Redington Award for Spirit and Excellence. Solo was presented the first Joe Redington Award for Outstanding Lead Dog. No dog before had ever displayed the initiative to move a team and an injured musher ahead as Solo had done. Solo could hear the reporters in the background using words like "legend" and "hero" attached to his name. Excited and stunned, he couldn't believe they were talking about him. Sela watched quietly from the clinic as Solo received his award. She thought of Teddy and how proud he would have been that their son was an Iditarod champion.

The Burled Arch rose above into the blue Nome sky as Harry, Solo, and all the team gathered for photos and interviews. Later that afternoon, when most of the commotion was over, Solo found himself looking back at the arch just at the same moment that a large raven flew beneath it, circled overhead and landed on the arch. "Thank you, Spirit," he whispered, finding himself running toward the arch, throwing himself into the air as if he could fly. At just that moment, with Solo still airborne, the raven flew down from the arch and touched the tip of Solo's ear with the tip of his wing. They were momentarily together in flight before Solo's feet reached the ground and the raven was gone.

THE END

GLOSSARY

Aurora Borealis – Another term for the northern lights – an atmospheric event that causes lights of many colors to swirl in the night sky.

Burled Arch – The Iditarod finish line in Nome.

Dog Booties – Cloth boots, usually with Velcro straps to hold them on. They are put on the feet of sled dogs to prevent injury on icy surfaces.

Duct Tape —A durable, silver cloth tape used widely to seal and repair items. An Alaska staple.

Fireweed – A tall, spiky, bright pink flowered stem that blooms all summer over much of Alaska.

Iditarod – A 1000-mile sled dog race starting in Anchorage, Alaska the first Saturday in March and winding through central and western Alaska wilderness until it ends in Nome, Alaska on the Bering Sea.

Iditarod Ceremonial Start – The first leg of the Iditarod race is run from Anchorage to Eagle River, Alaska – a suburb about 10 miles north of Anchorage. After this, the dogs and mushers are driven to Wasilla, Alaska, about 42 miles north of Anchorage for the real start of the race. The Ceremonial Start is when the mushers and their teams can mingle with the crowd and the media. The real race begins the next day in Wasilla.

Iditarod Start – The real start of the race has historically been in Wasilla, Alaska. Crowds of people line the streets to watch the mushers and their teams take off.

Joe Redington, Sr. – Known as the "Father of the Iditarod," he is credited with founding the first Iditarod race. He ran his last Iditarod at the age of 80 and has since passed away.

Lead Dog – The dog at the front of a sled dog team who leads the rest of the team.

Mandatory gear – Each musher in the Iditarod race is required to carry several mandatory survival items on his/her sled.

Musher –A person who drives a team of dogs pulling a sled.

Raven – A large, jet-black, crowlike bird of great symbolism in the culture of many Native Alaskan tribes.

Rookie – A musher running his first sled dog race.

Sled Dog – A mixed breed of dog bred for qualities of speed, strength, and endurance. Teams of 8 to 16 dogs pull mushers on their sleds.

Vi Redington – The widow of Joe Redington, Sr., still residing on the Iditarod trail in Knik, south of Wasilla.

Yukon Quest – Another famous dog race from Alaska to Canada

Blood Bank of Alaska's relationship with Joe Redington and his family began in 1997. In that year's Iditarod, Joe carried a unit of blood in honor of the Blood Bank's 35th Anniversary. Little did Joe realize the positive impact his role as spokesperson and ambassador for Alaska's only blood center would have on Alaskans. Blood awareness has improved, and the donation rates for the Blood Bank of Alaska's three centers have more than doubled. Joe once remarked, "I haven't ever given blood, but I know that it is a good thing to do." From that day on, Joe and his family have been committed to the Blood Bank of Alaska's mission. From delivering that unit of blood to Norton Sound Hospital in Nome in 1997 to receiving blood himself as part of his treatment prior to his death, Joe encouraged people to become blood donors. Following Joe's death in 1999, Raymie Redington, Joe's son, carried a package of limited edition commemorative envelopes for the Blood Bank. These envelopes, which each year feature a different musher, have been our gift since 1997 to our "Hero" donors, who express their dedication to their community by donating at least four times a year. Thanks to Joe, his family and all the mushers who have supported the Blood Bank of Alaska in the publication of this book. Thank you to those key staff of the Blood Bank who contributed so much of their personal time, especially Marianne and Dave. Finally, thank you to our loyal donors, who believe that giving the "Gift of Life" is the right thing to do.

Thomas K. Hathaway Ph.D
Chief Executive Officer
Blood Bank of Alaska